THE TEN COMMANDMENTS

A Text and Activity Book

By NANCY KARKOWSKY

Illustrated by Rabbi Jeffrey Sirkman

Games & Exercises by Sue Hurwitz

BEHRMAN HOUSE, INC.
PUBLISHERS

PROJECT EDITOR ADAM BENGAL

DESIGNER ROBERT O'DELL

Copyright © 1988 by Behrman House, Inc.
11 Edison Place, Sprringfield NJ 07081
www.behrmanhouse.com

ISBN 0-87441-477-6

Manufactured in the United States of America

THE TEN

COMMANDMENTS

Have you ever seen shapes like the ones on the left? They are two tablets.

These tablets symbolize, or remind us of, the Ten Commandments.

The Ten Commandments are ten laws that God gave to the Jewish people through Moses. They were carved on two tablets of stone long ago.

The Ten Commandments are very short because they do not use many words. The Ten Commandments are very big in what they teach us. They are very big in what they have done for the world.

The Ten Commandments help us to be Jewish.

The Ten Commandments help us to be good.

AT MOUNT SINAI

The Children of Israel were free! They had fled from cruel Pharaoh in Egypt and were slaves no more! The Sea of Reeds had split for them and they had escaped the pursuing armies.

Now Moses told them of a still greater miracle to come: In three days God would give them a special gift. There, right at the foot of Mount Sinai, God would give them ten laws, the Ten Commandments. The gift would make them a special people and a holy nation, forever and ever.

The Children of Israel felt great joy. A special gift from God! Young and old, men, women, and children, called out, with one voice and one heart:

"Na'aseh v'nishma"

"We will do and we will listen" We will do what God tells us to do.

Moses explained that everyone must bathe. Everyone must think fine, holy thoughts, and speak of fine, holy things, and make ready for the third day.

On the morning of the third day, everything was quiet.

Then suddenly, thunder roared, and lightning flashed. A thick, dark cloud covered the mountain. The call of a great shofar was heard. It grew louder and louder. Fire began to burn on the top of the mountain, and huge clouds of smoke rolled around the mountain.

The ground began to shake, and the people trembled. They felt as if they would fall.

Then all the Children of Israel—each and every one of them—heard the Voice of God.

Moses told them not to be afraid—that what they saw and heard this day would help them to remember and to obey God's commandments. But the people were frightened and stood far away. So Moses went up the mountain by himself, to hear God's words.

Moses stayed on the mountain for forty days and forty nights. Some of the people became afraid that he would never come back.

They forgot the promises they had made. They forgot God. They made a statue of gold—a golden calf—and began to pray to it, as if it were a god.

Moses came down the mountain, carrying two tablets of stone. On them were the Ten Commandments. He heard the people praying and singing to the golden calf, a statue. Moses became angry. The people didn't deserve the gift of the Ten

Commandments. He threw down the tablets, and they broke into many tiny pieces.

Then the Children of Israel realized what they had done—they had worshipped a statue instead of God. They begged Moses to forgive them. They asked for a second chance to learn and keep God's commandments.

Once again, Moses climbed up the mountain. Once again, he returned with the Ten Commandments carved on two tablets of stone. And once again, the Children of Israel, with a new joy, and more wisdom, promised to keep and honor the Ten Commandments, forever and ever.

CROSSWORD PUZZLE

Directions: Use these words to fill in
the puzzle below. GOLDEN CALF, MOUNT SINAI,
TEN COMMANDMENTS, STONE, SEA OF REEDS,
PHARAOH, SLAVES, MOSES

Across →
1. These laws help us to be Jewish.
3. The cruel _____ sent his armies after the Children of Israel.
5. Moses went up this mountain by himself, to hear God's words.
7. During the 40 days and 40 nights that Moses stayed on the mountain, the Children of Israel made a statue of a _____ _____.
9. The Children of Israel lived as _____ in Egypt.
11. The two tablets with the Ten Commandments were made of _____.

Down ↓
1. These laws help us to be good.
4. When the Children of Israel fled from Egypt, the _____ __ _____ split so they could escape.
6. _____ brought two tablets with the Ten Commandments down from Mount Sinai.

WORD SEARCH

Directions: The words listed below tell about the Children of Israel before they left Egypt and while they wandered in the desert. Circle them. (Hint: Answers may go down as well as across)

```
M I R A C L E S S T A S E A O F R E E D S T Y
K A N S A S R L N E W Y O R K X N O M L T Y Z
R E D S E A N A S I L V E R P H A N O A H N J
C A L I F O R V N I A C H I C A X Z U V B N M
J K L Y P K T E N L A W S A D K C L N B V P Q
J E R S E Y S R I N A I D E S E R T T R O H K
S T O N E T A Y L E T S S A M O S E S M O A N
T S T E N C O M M A N D M E N T S A I Q B R Z
O R G H A R O Z Y B V N C M X C O L N R A A O
N C O L T C A T W O T A B L E T S T A R E O Q
R E D B L U E G O L D E N C A L F Q I R S H N
```

TEN COMMANDMENTS   TWO TABLETS   MOUNT SINAI   MIRACLES   TEN LAWS
SLAVERY   MOSES   GOLDEN CALF   DESERT   PHARAOH   STONE   SEA OF REEDS

Can you think of ten laws that are very important for a people? Make up your own list.

1 _____

2 _____

3 _____

4 _____

5 _____

6 _____

7 _____

8 _____

9 _____

10 _____

"I am Adonai your God"

If you woke up one morning and saw the streets and sidewalks full of puddles, and the trees and grass dripping wet, what would you think?

You might think it had rained during the night. Even though you had not seen or heard the storm, you would know what had happened.

We believe in God in the same way that we believe there was a rainstorm during the night. Though we cannot see God, we see what God does in the world around us, and we know that God is there.

This kind of knowing and believing, even though we do not see something right in front of our eyes, is called *emunah*, or faith.

The first of the Ten Commandments tells us that we must believe in God: We have faith that God is One and that there is no other.

Sometimes it is easy to keep the First Commandment. Our faith is strong. Everything seems good and right in the world. We feel God's love and power.

Other times, it is more difficult. Nothing seems to go right. We cry "Where is God's love?"

The First Commandment tells us: no matter what happens, God is there, cares about us and takes care of us. God helps us in many ways, sometimes with great miracles like taking us out of Egypt. Sometimes with quieter miracles, like making it rain. Sometimes with the quietest miracle of all, the miracle of life.

We must always remember; we must always believe; we must always know: "I am Adonai your God."

The First Commandment also tells us where the other nine commandments came from and why we obey them.

They came from God. We obey them because they are God's laws.

A STORY

Once a prince came to a country and told the people, "I shall be your king."

The people were amazed. "What have you done for us that you should be our king?" they asked.

The prince did not answer, but went right to work. He dug a well so that the people would have water to drink. He plowed and planted so that they would have food to eat. He built a strong wall to protect them from their enemies.

Then once again he said to the people, "I shall be your king." This time they eagerly answered, "Yes, yes."

God acted the same way with the Children of Israel by taking them out of Egypt. No other people in history ever freed itself from slavery. When they wandered in the desert, God gave them water to drink and food to eat. God saved them from their enemies. Then when God said to them, "I am Adonai your God," the people remembered what God had done for them. They eagerly answered, "Na'aseh v'nishma."

MAZE

We believe in God in the same way we believe in what God does in the world around us. Trace the path of EMUNAH or FAITH that leads to the First Commandment in the maze below.

"I am Adonai your God"

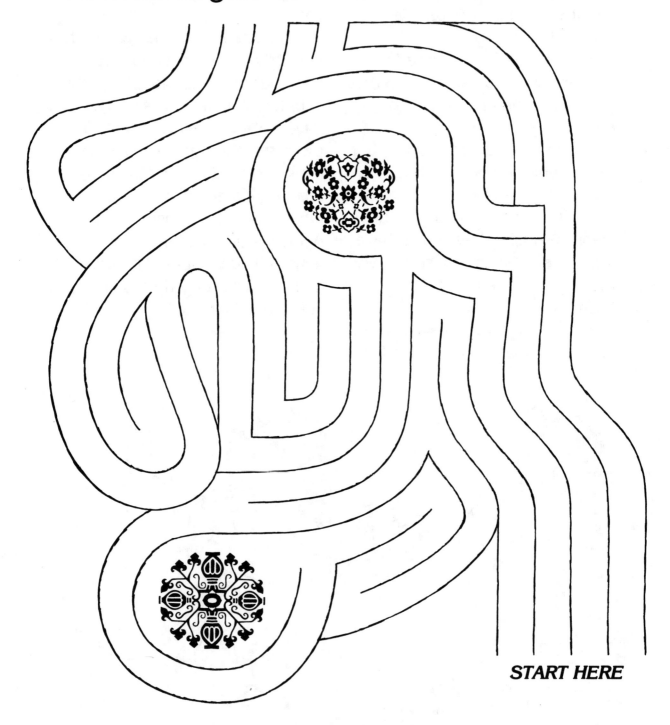

START HERE

MYSTERY WORD

Directions: Read each statement and decide if it is true or false. Circle the answer. Write the letter you circle on the correct line at the bottom of the page.

TRUE	FALSE

1 The first of the Ten Commandments tells us that we must believe in God.

2 EMUNAH is the belief in only what you can see or touch.

3 The First Commandment also tells us where the other nine commandments came from and why we obey them.

4 Though we cannot see God, we see what God does in the world.

5 The Ten Commandments are God's laws.

TRUE	FALSE
F	B
R	A
I	T
T	S
H	W

MYSTERY WORD:

_____ _____ _____ _____ _____
   1   2   3   4   5

THINGS TO DO

Trace and cut out the shape on this page. Cut along the diagonal lines, but be careful not to cut through the middle.

Fold one corner of each triangle down to the dot in the middle. Carefully stick a straight pin or tack through the dot to make a pinwheel. Stick into the eraser of a pencil.

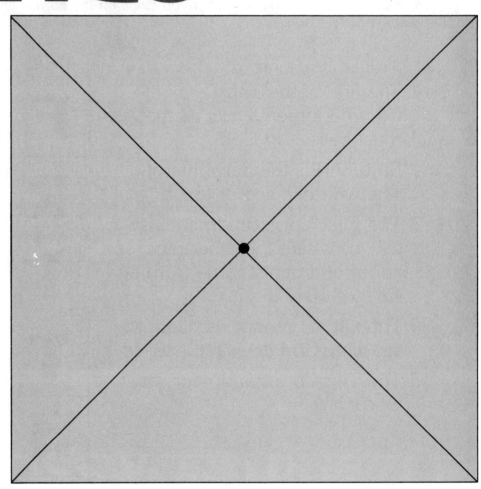

FOLD AND TAPE

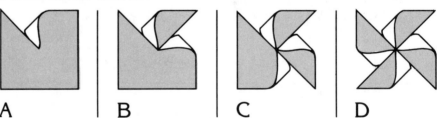

A | B | C | D

Blow on your pinwheel. What makes the pinwheel spin? Can you
see the air that turns it? Can you feel or hear or touch the air?
How do you know that there is air, even though you cannot see
it?

_____

_____

_____

How is this like God?

_____

_____

_____

Why do you think "I am Adonai your God" is the first of the Ten
Commandments?

_____

_____

_____

_____

"You shall have no other gods beside Me"

Long ago people worshipped statues of wood and stone called idols. The people thought that idols were gods.

The Second Commandment tells us it is wrong to worship idols. There is only one God. We must not worship false gods. We remember this every time we say the *Shema*:

"Hear, O Israel: Adonai is our God, Adonai is One".

Many people, even whole nations, do not follow this commandment. They may not make statues of wood or stone, but they do make "gods" of things,

or ideas, or people. They act as if these things or ideas or people were gods.

Some people worship money or power. They will do anything—even cheat or steal—to get rich or famous or important.

Whenever people think something is more important than doing what is right, they are making it into a god.

There is only one God. We must worship God, and God alone. If we worship other things or people, we are worshiping idols.

A STORY

Abraham tried to decide what he should worship. He saw a star.

"Perhaps I should worship that star?" Abraham thought.

But then the moon rose, and it was bigger and brighter than the star.

"Perhaps I should worship the moon?" Abraham thought.

But then the sun came up, and it was larger and brighter than the moon and the stars.

"Perhaps I should worship the sun?" Abraham thought.

But evening came, and the sun went down.

"There must be a God who created the stars, the moon, and the sun, and is greater than all of them. That is the God I will worship."

When he said that, Abraham became the first Jew, and his children after him the Jewish people.

20

MAZE

"You shall have no other gods beside Me"

The Second Commandment tells us it is wrong to worship idols. There is only one God. We must not worship false gods. Trace the path around the false gods of idols, money, and power that some people worship to find the way to the Second Commandment.

START HERE

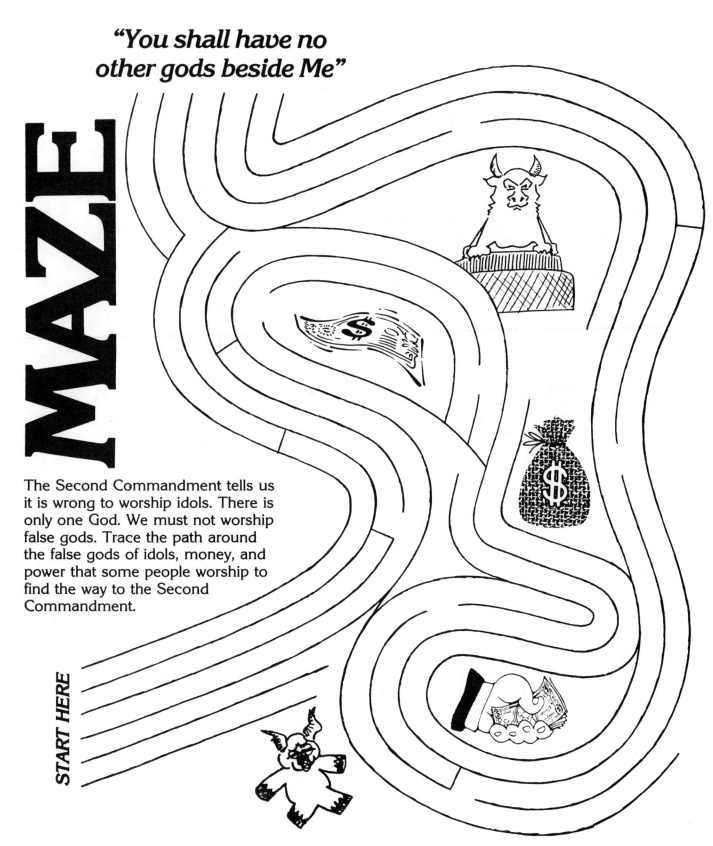

CATEGORY SORT

Directions:
A category is a group of things, or words, that go together. The words listed below tell about either the First Commandment or the Second Commandment.
Write the number of the correct commandment in the circle next to each word.

Faith

No worship of idols

No other gods

Shema

Believing

What God does in the world around us

"Hear, O Israel: Adonai is our God, Adonai is One"

No worship of money or power

Emunah

22

THINGS TO THINK ABOUT

1

An American general once said,
"My country, right or wrong."
How was he going against the Second Commandment?

_____

_____

_____

_____

_____

_____

2

The general was trying to be
loyal to his country. What do you think
he should have said?

_____

_____

_____

_____

_____

_____

"You shall not take the Name of the Adonai your God in vain"

COMMANDMENT

The Third Commandment is about keeping promises: promises made in God's Name. A promise in God's Name is a vow. If we break that promise, we have taken God's Name in vain.

All of us know how good we feel when someone keeps a promise. We also know how bad we feel when someone breaks a promise.

Promises are just as important to the Jewish people. The Jewish people promised that they would learn and keep the Ten Commandments. God promised that the Jewish people would be a great and holy nation.

When two people get married, they promise to take care of, and to care for, each other.

When young men or women become *bar* or *bat mitzva,* they promise to be responsible Jewish adults.

Every year, on Rosh Hashana and Yom Kippur, we all promise to try to be good in the coming year.

A promise made in God's Name is sacred. But, whether we use God's Name or not, we must always try to keep our promises, as good Jews, and as good people.

FROM THE BIBLE

Abraham's servant, Eliezer, had sworn that he would find a good wife for Abraham's son, Isaac. But as he traveled, he worried. Would he be able to keep his promise? He prayed to God to help him.

As he came near the city of Haran in the land of Mesopotamia, Rebekah came out to the well to get water for her family. Eliezer ran to her and asked, "Please give me a little water from your pitcher."

Rebekah hurried to give him water. "Drink as much as you need," she said. "Then I will bring water for your camels."

As Rebekah hurried back and forth with the heavy pitcher of water, Eliezer said a prayer. He thanked God, for he saw that Rebekah would be a good wife for Isaac, and that he could keep his promise to his master, Abraham.

FROM THE TALMUD

Before God gave the Ten Commandments to the Jewish people, God offered these laws to other nations. The other nations asked what the laws were. When they heard, they refused them. One nation would not accept a law that told them not to murder and another nation would not obey a law that told them not to steal.

But the Jewish people did not ask what the Ten Commandments were. With one heart and one voice, they called out, "Na'aseh v'nishma." "We will do and we will listen." They accepted God's Law without question.

NA'ASEH v'NISHMAH

CROSSWORD PUZZLE

Directions: Use these words to fill in the puzzle below.
VAIN, ROSH HASHANAH AND YOM KIPPUR, PROMISES, BAR OR BAT MITZVAH, TEN COMMANDMENTS, CARE, VOW

Across→

1. The Third Commandment is about keeping _____ .
3. When two people marry they promise to _____ for each other.
5. Every year, on _____ _____, we all promise to try to be good in the coming year.
7. When young men or women become _____ _____, they promise to be responsible Jewish adults.

Down ↓

2. The Jewish people promised they would learn and keep the _____ _____ .
4. A promise in God's Name is a _____ .
6. If we break a vow, we have taken God's Name in _____ .

WORD SEARCH

```
O O D T H I R D C O M B A W D W
T H I R D C O M M A N D M E N T
N W O N T A L L O W I T X W N D
Q W R G O O D X V M A Z I I X Y
Z V A H B A R M A R R I A L E O
V P R O M I S E S Q W Y R L L M
V W E W O R L D H E A R I D P K
X G D W I L L W A N T U S O T I
R O S H H A S H A N A N A H X P
R O B A T Y O M R O S H K I P P
G D O O D E S P U N S A B L E U
B A R O R B A T M I T Z V A H R
Y U A R E S P O N S I B L E F O
C A R E A B O U T E A C H O T H
C O M M A N D M M E N T O N E O
G H J W Q P O M A R R I A G E B
W Q T Y U S E C O N D L I S T E
W E W I L L L I S T E N V O W S
```

Directions: The words listed on the left tell about keeping promises made in God's Name. Circle them. (Hint: Answers may go down as well as across)

THIRD COMMANDMENT
CARE
MARRIAGE
BAR OR BAT MITZVAH
PROMISES
VOWS
WE WILL LISTEN
WE WILL DO
ROSH HASHANAH
YOM KIPPUR
GOOD
RESPONSIBLE

Why is a promise more than just saying some words? Why is keeping a promise important?

_____

_____

_____

Why is a promise in God's Name even more important?

_____

_____

_____

"Remember the Sabbath day and keep it holy"

Did you ever count the days until a special day came—a birthday or a holiday?

The Jewish people have a holiday every week. It is called the Sabbath, which means Day of Rest. We also call that day the "Sabbath Queen," and welcome her into our homes on Friday night.

As the sun begins to set on Friday evening, we light the Sabbath candles and bless them. *Kiddush,* the blessing over the wine, welcomes the Sabbath Queen, too. *Hamotzi,* the blessing over bread, begins the Sabbath meal and makes it holy. After the meal, we sing songs and blessings, thanking God for everything.

The day of the Sabbath Queen is a time to do happy things. We walk and talk with family. We visit with friends. We read and think to ourselves. We go to the synagogue to pray, to read from the Torah and to think about what it means to be Jewish. We rest from the work of the week.

The ending of the Sabbath day is quiet and a little sad. We are sorry it is over, but we know that the Sabbath Queen will return in six days. So we remember the Sabbath day that we just had, and count the days until she returns once again.

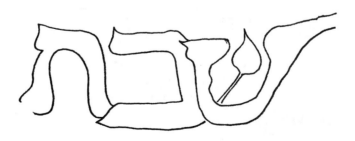

A STORY

Rabbi Judah was concerned. Whenever the emperor visited him before, he had been able to prepare a fine meal, a meal fit for a king. But today was the Sabbath, and he could not cook. The meal had to be simple and cold. But he did not have to worry.

"Ah," sighed the emperor, very pleased, "though I have been in your home for many meals, Rabbi Judah, this meal has been the tastiest. What spice did you use to give it such flavor?"

Rabbi Judah smiled.

"The spice is the Sabbath, my lord. It gives flavor to everything it touches."

A LEGEND

Once a man bought an ox to help him plow. The ox worked well for six days, but on Saturday, it would not go out into the fields.

The man sent for the person who had sold him the ox. The former owner apologized. "Saturday is my Sabbath," he explained. "The ox is used to resting on this day."

The new owner decided that if an ox could understand the Sabbath, he should learn more about it himself. This he did, and one day he became a great rabbi.

FROM THE TALMUD

After God had created the world and all that is in it, the Sabbath day began to weep.

"All the days of the week have partners," she cried, "except for me. The first day has the second day; the third day has the fourth day; the fifth day has the sixth day. Only I, the seventh day, am left alone."

God comforted the Sabbath Queen: "You are not alone. The Jewish people will be your partner."

When God gave the Jewish people the Ten Commandments,

Then God told the Jewish people, "At the beginning of the world, I promised the Sabbath Queen that she would be your bride. Now I command you: Remember the Sabbath day to keep it holy."

34

A LEGEND

Friday night, two angels come to visit every Jewish home, a Sabbath angel and a dark angel.

If the Sabbath table is set and the candles lit, if the home glows with happiness and peace, the Sabbath angel joyfully says, "May it be like this every Sabbath." Then the dark angel must reply: "Amen: May it be always so."

If the Sabbath is forgotten, and the home is dark with unhappiness and quarrels, the dark angel rejoices: "May it be like this every Sabbath." Then the Sabbath angel must reply, "Amen: May it always be so."

CROSSWORD PUZZLE

Directions: Use these words to fill in the puzzle below.
SABBATH QUEEN, FOURTH COMMANDMENT, PRAY, DAY OF REST, TORAH, KIDDUSH, FRIDAY NIGHT, HAMOTZI

Down ↓

1. "Remember the Sabbath Day to Keep it Holy" is the _____ _____.
3. On Shabbat we go to our synagogue or temple to _____.
5. Another name for Shabbat is the _____ _____.
7. Shabbat begins when the sun sets on _____ _____.
9. The blessing over wine is called _____.

Across →

2. The blessing over bread is called _____.
4. The _____ is read in synagogues and temples on Shabbat morning.
6. Another name for Shabbat is _____ of _____.

WORD SEARCH

Directions: The words listed below tell about how we

"Remember the Sabbath Day to keep it Holy."

Circle them. (Hint: Answers may go down as well as across)

```
K I A G S A B B A T H Q U E E N M P
I F O U R T H C O M M A N D M E N T
D A Y O F R E S T D A Y O F D E L E
D B I M A H A R K E T Y R N P X Z M
U V I S I T S I D D U R T A L L I P
S S A B B A T H D A Y P R A Y T R L
H A M O T Z I W A L K T A L K V I E
T O D A T O R A H S Y N T U V W X Y
V C X Z S D R A H J K W Q E R P L J
W O N Q A L L S Y N A G O G U E M N
```

KIDDUSH   HAMOTZI   SABBATH QUEEN   DAY OF REST

FOURTH COMMANDMENT   SYNAGOGUE   TEMPLE   PRAY

TORAH   SABBATH DAY

A family wants to welcome the Sabbath.
Below is a list of things they could
put on the table. Cross out those that are
not necessary for the Sabbath.

a cloth to cover the challah   tablecloth   prayerbook   the evening paper

cake   two candlesticks with candles   napkins   kiddush cup

ice cream   bottle of pop   two loaves of challah   chicken soup

Torah scroll   colored dishes   bottle of wine   a crossword puzzle

lollipops   a Sunday School book

How is preparing
for the Sabbath
on Friday night
like preparing
for the visit of
a queen?

"Honor your father and your mother"

Life is a precious gift, the most precious gift we ever receive. God gave life to the first man and woman, Adam and Eve. Our parents gave life to us, their children. Our life is a partnership between our parents and God.

The Fifth Commandment tells us to honor our parents as we honor God. To "honor" our parents means to treat them with respect.

Though we love our parents, and they love us, we may sometimes disagree with them, and feel we don't want to do what they say. But honoring our parents means to always speak and act nicely to them.

Honoring our parents is a very special way to thank them, and God, for a very precious gift: our life.

A RIDDLE

Once there were two men, sons of two fathers. One man served his father a fine meal, but did not keep the Fifth Commandment. The second man made his father work in his mill, but he did keep the Fifth Commandment. How was this possible?

Answer: The first man served his father some expensive food. When the father asked his son where he got such fine food, the son answered, "Shut up, old man, and eat."

The second man heard that the government was taking men to work in mills. He knew the bosses might be harsh to the workers. He said to his father, "You stay here and work in my mill, and I will go to work in the government mill. If they speak roughly, they will speak roughly to me; if they beat someone, they will beat me. I would rather I suffer than you."

WORD SORT

(Hint: Look back on page 40 if you need to.)

CLUES

1. Life is a _____ gift.

2. "_____ your father and your mother".

3. God created Adam, the first _____ .

4. God created Eve, the first _____ .

5. Honoring our parents is a very _____ way to thank them, and God, for our being alive.

6. Our _____ gave life to us.

7. _____ should always speak and act nicely to their parents even when they disagree.

8. The _____ precious gift we ever receive is life.

9. To "honor" our parents means to _____ as if they are special.

10. Our being alive is a _____ between our parents and God.

11. To "honor" our parents also means to _____ them, and to be polite.

Directions: The words below tell about the Fifth Commandment, **"Honor Your Father and Your Mother."** Use them to fill in the blank spaces. HONOR, RESPECT, BEHAVE, CHILDREN, SPECIAL, PARTNERSHIP, MOST, PRECIOUS, MAN, WOMAN, PARENTS

COMMANDMENT

1 _ _ _ _____ _____

2 _ _____ _____

3 _ _____ _____

4 _ _____ _____

5 _ _ _ _____ _____

6 _ _ _____ _____

7 _ _ _ _____ _____

8 _ _____ _____

9 _ _ _ _ _____ _____

10 _ _ _ _ _____ _____

11 _ _ _ _ _ _____

43

_____ Commandment

Day of Rest
Pray
Sabbath Day
Hamotzi
Kiddush

_____ Commandment

Faith
Emunah
I am The Lord Your God
Believing
What God does in the
world around us

CATEGORY REVIEW

Directions: The words in each list tell about one of the first five Commandments. Write the number of the Commandment in the space above each list. (Hint: Look back on pages 11, 18, 24, 30, and 40 if you need to.)

_____ Commandment

No other gods
No worship of money
No worship of power
No worship of people
No worship of idols

_____ Commandment

Honor Father and Mother
Life
Parents
Children
Partnership with God

_____ Commandment

Promises made in God's name
Sacred
Vow
Promise to try to be good
Promise to be responsible
Jewish adults

About the riddle

How did the man who owned a mill honor his father?
How could the man who served the delicious meal also
have honored his father?

_____

_____

_____

How did your parents honor their parents?

_____

_____

_____

_____

How do you honor your parents when you visit
your grandparents?

_____

_____

_____

_____

"You shall not murder"

We thank God for the gift of life—our lives and other peoples' lives. We do not take that great gift from another person. No one is permitted to hurt someone else.

Life is a precious gift. Just as we would not wish anyone to take away our life, no one should take away anyone else's life.

Killing another human being is a terrible crime. It is called murder. The Sixth Commandment forbids murder.

Every person is considered a whole world. To destroy that person is to destroy children that might have been born and things that might have been accomplished.

"If a person saves one life, it is as if a whole world had been saved. If a person destroys one life, it is as if a whole world had been destroyed," says our Talmud.

A STORY FROM THE TALMUD

The Children of Israel had just crossed the Sea of Reeds on dry land. The Egyptian soldiers chasing them had drowned. Great waves rolled in to cover them.

In their joy at being saved, the Israelites burst into song:
"I will sing because God has completely triumphed:
The horse and its rider God has hurled into the sea. . . ."

The angels in heaven saw the great miracle, and they too began to sing. But God stopped them with sad, stern words.

"The Egyptians are also My creatures. How can you sing when My children are dying?"

A LEGEND

Once there was a great king who put statues of himself all over his land.

The people of the land became angry. They wanted to rebel against the king. They could not touch him in his castle high above them, so they knocked down his statues and smashed them.

The king was sad. He knew that the people's anger and hatred were really meant for him, not for the statues.

In the same way, God is sad when one person kills another, knowing that the murderer rebels against God's law, "You shall not murder."

A STORY

Hillel was a poor boy who wanted, more than anything else in the world, to study the Torah.

One cold Friday afternoon, he finished his job of gathering wood. He climbed onto the roof of the Jewish school and lay by the window. He could hear the words of the rabbis. He listened so carefully that he did not notice that it began to snow. The snow covered him like a soft, thick blanket.

Inside the school, it became dark—time to light the candles for Shabbat. The rabbis looked up and saw the shape of a boy against the window in the roof.

They rushed to bring the half-frozen boy into the school. They built a fire to warm him. The students were amazed to see their teachers working so hard on the Sabbath. The rabbis explained.

''Life is so precious, that we may work on the Sabbath to save someone's life.''

CROSSWORD PUZZLE

Directions: Use these words to fill in the puzzle below.
PERSON, WORLD, MURDER, SIXTH COMMANDMENT, LIFE, HUMAN

Down ↓

1. The _____ _____ forbids murder.
3. To destroy a _____ is to destroy his world.

Across→

2. We thank God for the gift of _____.
4. Killing another _____ being is a terrible crime.
6. If a person saves one life it is as if he had saved the whole _____.
8. "You Shall Not _____".

In the picture below, the Jewish people are singing because God saved them from the Egyptian soldiers who were chasing them.

Draw the sea in front of them. Color the water, the land and the sky.

Why did God stop the angels from singing after the Jewish People had been saved?

_____

_____

_____

_____

_____

_____

_____

"You shall not commit adultery"

The word "adultery" in the Seventh Commandment has nothing to do with acting like an adult. It comes from the same root as "adulterate," which means to spoil or ruin. A person who commits adultery spoils or ruins a marriage by taking away someone else's husband or wife.

Marriages and families are very important to the Jewish people. A person who commits adultery breaks up a home, and takes a parent away from children. A marriage is ruined, and many people are hurt, even God.

A STORY

Once there were a husband and wife who loved each other very much, but had no children. They decided that they would leave each other and marry other people. Then perhaps they would each be blessed with children.

They told the rabbi, and he said, "You had a celebration when you got married. Now have a celebration before you leave each other."

The two went home and had a wonderful meal and celebrated together. Afterwards the husband told his wife to take with her the one thing she loved most in the house. Then he went to sleep.

While he slept, his wife had the servants carry him to her new home. The next day the husband awoke in a strange bed.

"What is this?" he cried. "Where am I?"

"You said that I could take the one thing I love most," his wife answered. "The thing I love most is you."

Then the couple realized that they should not leave each other, but should stay married to each other. The wise rabbi prayed for their happiness together, and not long afterwards they had a child.

FROM THE BIBLE

Long ago, when men were allowed to have more than one wife, King David had several wives. His neighbor, Uriah the Hittite, had only one wife. Her name was Bathsheba. She was very beautiful.

Once, when Uriah was away from home, King David told his servants to bring Bathsheba to his palace. He kept her there.

Many days later, Nathan the prophet came to the king. "My lord," Nathan said, "I know a rich man who has many sheep. His neighbor, a poor man, had only one little lamb that he loved dearly. One day, the rich man took away the lamb that the poor man loved so. What do you think should be done?"

King David was furious. "That rich man deserves to die," he roared. "Tell him to give his neighbor four lambs for the one he took away."

Then Nathan told David, "You are the rich man, and Uriah the poor man. Though you had many wives, you took Bathsheba. Now Uriah is dead, and you cannot give him anything."

Then David realized the terrible wrong he had done. "I have sinned," he said. He fasted and prayed that God would not give him the punishment he deserved.

HEBREW LETTERS

The Hebrew word for "fire" is aish. The Hebrew word for "man" is ish. The Hebrew word for "woman" is isha. The Hebrew letters yud and hay change the word "fire" into the words "man" or "woman." They also are a way to write God's name.

If a man and woman honor each other and keep God's commandments, God is with them, and all is well. If a man and woman do not honor each other, God is not with them, and there is "fire" between them—anger, pain, and sadness.

A BIBLE STORY

Hosea the prophet had a wife who committed adultery. He was hurt, angry, and upset. He did not know what to do. God understood how Hosea felt, because the Jewish people were not always faithful.

God spoke to Hosea and said that the Jewish people also "commit adultery" when they worship other gods.

God told Hosea that everything would be all right when the Jewish people returned to God, and when Hosea's wife returned to him: "She shall say, 'I will return to my first husband, for then it was better with me than now'" (Hosea 2:9).

Then God will say to the Jewish people, and Hosea will say to his wife: "I will marry you forever . . . in righteousness, and in justice, and in kindness, and in mercy . . . and in faithfulness . . ." (Hosea 2:21–22).

WORD SEARCH

Directions: The words listed below tell about the Bible story of the Seventh Commandment,

"You shall not commit adultery."

Circle them. (Hint: Answers may go down as well as across)

```
O N E L I T T L E L A M B S H A L L
N O T K I N G D A V I D T O W L A R
L A R G E A G O A T S T H R E E C A
T S C X Q T O N E M A N Y S H E E P
A B R N Y H D F L L O A F N I M A L
U R I A H A M N O P Q W R C H W P T
S I X T H N S E V E N T U H C O M M
D R E B J K Q R F F A M I L Y H I L
A D U L T E R Y L O V E N A D U L T
Q W T Y M A R R I A G E O N R K S V
K I T C H E N B A T H S H E B A S I
```

BATHSHEBA   KING DAVID   URIAH   NATHAN   LOVE

FAMILY   MARRIAGE   ADULTERY   RUIN   MANY SHEEP   ONE LITTLE LAMB

60

MYSTERY WORD

Directions: Read each statement and decide if it is true or false. Circle the answer. Write the letter you circle on the correct line at the bottom of the page.

	TRUE	FALSE
1 "You Shall Not Commit Adultery" is the Eighth Commandment.	S	R
2 The word adultery comes from a root word meaning to spoil or ruin.	U	N
3 When a marriage is ruined, even God is hurt.	I	R
4 Marriages and families have never been important to Jewish people.	B	N

MYSTERY WORD:

_____ _____ _____ _____
   1   2   3   4

THINGS

*In the space below,
draw a family.*

TO DO

How did God comfort Hosea the prophet?

_____

_____

_____

_____

How should a man and woman act towards each other to protect their family?

_____

_____

_____

_____

"You shall not steal"

We learned it is wrong to take someone else's husband or wife. It is also wrong to take *anything* that belongs to someone else. Taking something that does not belong to you is called stealing.

There are many ways to take something that is not ours. Robbery, mugging and shop-lifting are some of the ways. Cheating or lying are ways to steal someone else's knowledge or ideas. Kidnapping means stealing people.

Just as we would not want someone to take anything that belongs to us, we must never take anything that belongs to anyone else. Whether we take their things, their thoughts, or themselves, we are stealing.

FROM THE TALMUD

The students of Rabbi Simon ben Shetach bought him a donkey. After they had brought it to his home, they found a jewel hidden in its coat.

"You must return the jewel to the person who sold you the donkey," the rabbi told them.

"Why?" asked the students. "No one will ever know where you got the jewel."

"You will know, I will know, God will know," answered the rabbi. "If we do not return the jewel, we will be taking something that does not belong to us. Neither I nor my students shall be thieves," he said.

"Return the jewel to the man who sold you the donkey. He will say, 'Blessed be the God of the Jews.' That blessing is worth more to me than all the jewels in the world."

A STORY

The conqueror Alexander the Great was visiting the court of King Katzya beyond the dark mountain. Two men came into the court. One had just bought a field from the other, and found a treasure in it. He wanted to return the treasure because it did not belong to him. The former owner would not take the treasure, because it did not belong to him.

King Katzya asked Alexander what he would do. The conqueror laughed.

"My answer is simple. I would take the treasure for myself."

"But it does not belong to you," cried the king.

Alexander smiled. "What will you do?" he asked.

King Katzya turned to one of the men. "Do you have a son?"

"Yes," the man answered.

King Katzya turned to the other man. "Do you have a daughter?"

"Yes," said the man.

"Let the son marry the daughter. The treasure will be their wedding present," Katzya decreed.

CROSSWORD PUZZLE

Directions: Use these words to fill in the puzzle below.
KIDNAPPING, ADULTERY, MURDER, STEALING, CHEATING, LYING

Across→

1. Taking someone else's husband or wife is called _____ .
3. Taking something that does not belong to you is called _____ .
5. _____ is a way to steal someone else's knowledge or ideas.
7. _____ is another way to steal someone else's knowledge or ideas.

Down ↓

2. Stealing people is called _____ .
4. Killing another human being is called _____ .

WORD SEARCH

Directions: Circle the words listed below that tell about actions forbidden by the Commandments: (Hint: Answers may go down as well as across)

6th "You shall not murder"
7th "You shall not commit adultery"
8th "You shall not steal"

STEALING
KIDNAPPING
CHEATING
LYING
SHOP-LIFTING
ADULTERY
MURDER
KILLING
MUGGING
ROBBERY

```
Q W P U Y S H O P P I N G M R D E Z X
K I L L I N G S H O P - L I F T I N G
S T E Y Y U S H L L N T C O M M I T Q
S T L I N A R O B B E R Y I W T Y P U
K I D N A P P I N G S H A L L N O T T
A M U G R D R C H T S H C P L F T N G
D O N T D O I T Y O U S H A L L N O T
U S D G H J X V N M S T E A L I N G A
L Q B V X X Z B J Y U R A P U Q T W C
T B M U R O B B K I D O T N A P P I N
E M U G G I N G L Y I N I K X Z B M P
R R R E S T E A A Q W R T N Y B V X C Y
Y S Y M U R D E R I S N G V R Y N C E
```

THINGS TO THINK ABOUT

Is it right for a poor person to steal?

What should we do so a poor person
does not have to steal?

_____

_____

_____

_____

What do you think of the saying,
"Finders keepers, losers weepers?

_____

_____

_____

_____

Should a person expect a reward
for returning something that was lost?

_____

_____

_____

_____

"You shall not bear false witness"

A "witness" is someone who has seen something happen. To "bear witness" means to tell about something you saw.

For example, the Jewish people witnessed the giving of the Ten Commandments. We testify to that in the Torah.

To "bear false witness" means to tell about something that you never saw, to lie. The Ninth Commandment tells us never to lie.

Lies cause great pain and unhappiness. Because of lies, innocent people are punished.

But when everyone tells the truth, we know that justice will be done, and that people can live together in peace.

The Talmud says: "The world exists because of three things: Truth, Justice, and Peace" (*Ethics of the Fathers,* 1:18).

A FABLE

Dark clouds hung overhead. The rain would soon fall, and bring the Great Flood. Two by two, the creatures of the world entered the ark so they would be saved with Noah and his family.

In came Truth and Peace. Then came Love and Good Deeds. Lies tried to sneak in by himself, but was stopped at the door; he must have a partner to enter the ark.

Madly he dashed out into the darkness. Soon he returned with an evil grin on his face and Wickedness at his side. Wickedness had agreed to be Lies' mate and to come with him on the ark. But any good that Lies gained was grabbed by Wickedness every time.

PAIRS ONLY
PLEASE PRESENT
2 FORMS
OF IDENTIFICATION

PACK OF
LIES

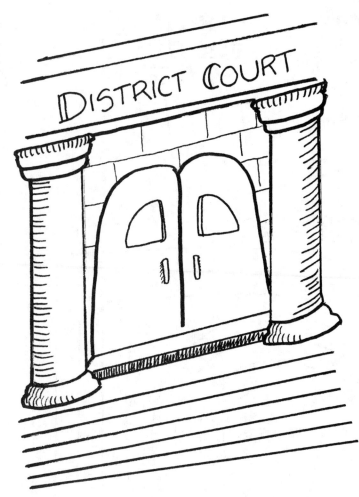

A STORY

One day a student met his teacher near the court of law. The teacher asked the student for help.

"Will you be a witness for my law case?" the teacher asked.

"How can I do that?" the student asked. "I do not know what happened."

"That person owes me money," answered the teacher. "I would not lie to you. You simply tell the court what I am telling you. It is the truth."

"I am sorry, but I cannot be a witness," replied the student. "I am sure that you are telling me the truth, but I did not see anything. If I say I did—even if you are telling the truth—I will be bearing false witness, and that is not right."

MAZE

Trace the path around actions *forbidden* by
our first nine Commandments to find the way to:

**TRUTH
JUSTICE
PEACE**

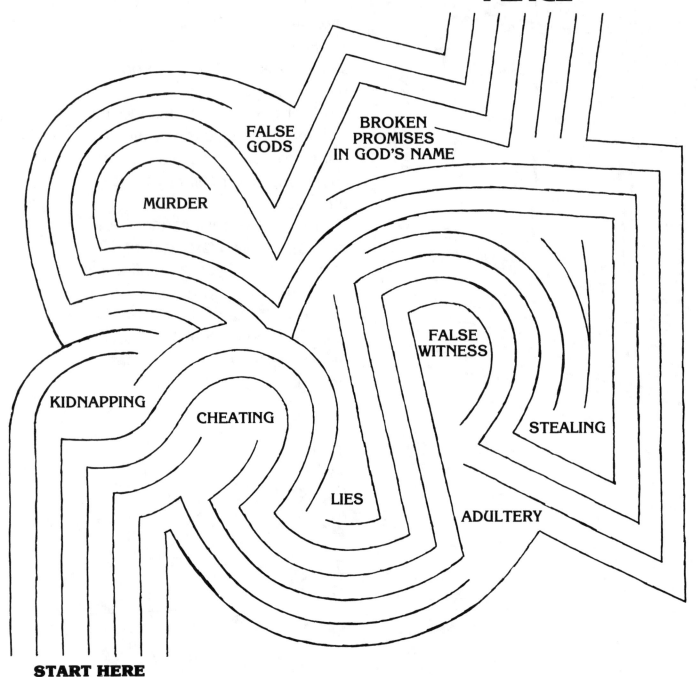

FALSE
GODS

BROKEN
PROMISES
IN GOD'S NAME

MURDER

FALSE
WITNESS

KIDNAPPING

CHEATING

STEALING

LIES

ADULTERY

START HERE

A WORD GAME

Unscramble the words on the left and write them in the spaces on the right. You can find the words at the right side of the page, unscrambled, but in a different order.

JUSTICE
LIE
JUST
JUDGE
COURT
GUILTY
CASE
RIGHT
WITNESS
PEACE
TRUTH
WRONG

GROWN

SSNETIW

GIRTH

GUJED

TROUC

SEAC

TUIGLY

TUSJ

ILE

ICEJUST

THTRU

CEAEP

CATEGORY SORT

Directions: The words listed below tell about the Eighth and Ninth Commandments. Write the number of the correct Commandment above each word.

8th "You Shall Not Steal"
9th "You Shall Not Bear False Witness"

_____
False witness

_____
Lies against someone else

_____
Taking something that belongs to anyone else

_____
Lies to steal someone's knowledge or ideas

_____
Stealing

_____
Lies that punish innocent people

_____
Justice

_____
Telling the truth about something you saw

_____
Truth

_____
Peace

Should one lie to help a friend?

_____

_____

_____

_____

_____

What is the difference between
making up an imaginary story
and telling a lie?

_____

_____

_____

_____

_____

"You shall not covet"

If you think about it, the list of things we really need in this world is not very long. We could count our real needs on our fingers, maybe even one hand.

Our "wants," though, are another story. There is no end to the things we might like to have.

The Tenth Commandment is about wanting something too much—something someone else has. To want something that belongs to someone else is to "covet," and the Tenth Commandment tells us that is wrong.

To want something, even very much, is not wrong, if we are willing to work hard and honestly to earn it. To covet is wrong, though, when we are jealous of someone else who has something and we would like to take it away. It is wrong if we want something so much that we would be willing to do something wrong to get it, like lie, steal, or break one of the Ten Commandments.

FROM THE BIBLE

King Ahab had many fields, but he coveted a field that belonged to his neighbor, Naboth. He wanted that field so much that he could not eat or sleep, thinking about it.

Ahab's wife, Queen Jezebel, decided to get the field for him. She ordered two men to bear false witness against Naboth in court. They swore he had committed a great crime. Naboth was killed, and Ahab got the field.

Elijah, the prophet, heard how King Ahab had coveted what belonged to Naboth. Elijah saw how coveting had led to false witness, to killing, and to stealing. He told Ahab and Jezebel that they would be punished. They would die bloody deaths, and their children would not rule after them.

His words came true.

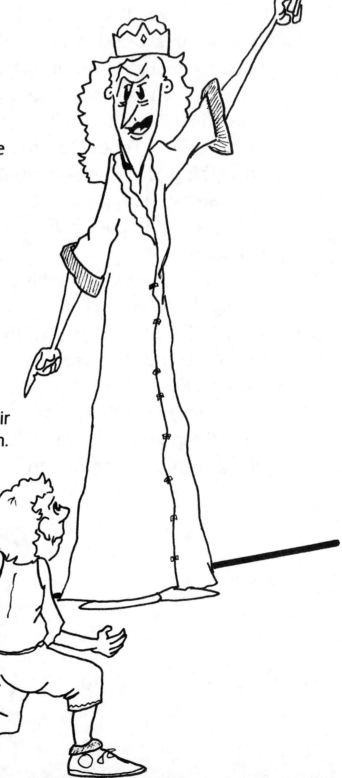

A FABLE

Many children gathered in the middle of town with sacks in their hands. Each sack held the good things that each child owned. There and then, a child could trade his sack for anyone else's.

Joseph looked around. He would have liked to have Ruth's sack of books, but he did not want to give her his sack of toys.

Ruth would have liked Malki's pretty dresses, but she did not want to give Malki her sack of books.

Malki wished she could have Shulamit's new shoes, but she did not want to give away her own dresses.

By the end of the day, no one had traded with anyone else. Every child went home with the same sack he or she had brought.

CROSSWORD PUZZLE

Directions: Use these words to fill in the puzzle below.
NEEDS, WANTS, EARN, TENTH COMMANDMENT,
JEALOUS, COVET

Across →

1. The _____ _____ says
   it is wrong to want something so much
   that we would be willing to break one
   of the Ten Commandments to get it.
3. To want something, even very much, is
   not wrong if we are willing to
   _____ it honestly.
5. Our list of "_____" in this
   world is not very long.

Down ↓

2. When we covet something that someone
   else has and we would like to take it away,
   we are _____.
4. To want something that belongs
   to someone else is to _____.
6. Our "_____" are things we might
   like to have.

WORD FUN

Fill in the missing letters in the words below. Then put the letters in the right order. Then you will know how we feel when we are happy with what we have, and do not covet anything.

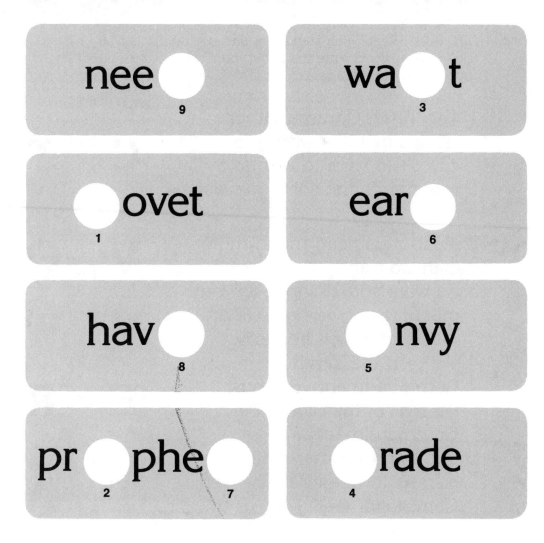

nee◯ 9

wa◯t 3

◯ovet 1

ear◯ 6

hav◯ 8

◯nvy 5

pr◯phe◯ 2   7

◯rade 4

___ ___ ___ ___ ___ ___ ___ ___ ___
1   2   3   4   5   6   7   8   9

List: prophet   have   trade   want   need   earn   envy   covet

MYSTERY WORD

Directions: Read each statement and decide if it is true or false. Circle the answer. Write the letter you circle on the correct line at the bottom of the page.

	TRUE	FALSE
1 The Tenth Commandment tells us that it is wrong to covet—to want to take away something that someone else has.	**C**	**T**
2 Most of us need much more than we want.	**V**	**O**
3 To want something, even very much, is not wrong if we are willing to earn it honestly.	**V**	**W**
4 To keep the Tenth Commandment you must keep all of the other nine Commandments.	**E**	**R**
5 The Ten Commandments help us to be good. The Ten Commandments help us to be Jewish.	**T**	**A**

MYSTERY WORD:

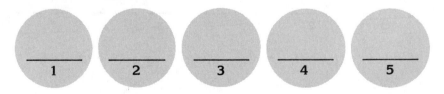

    1   2   3   4   5

Make a list of the things you need to live.

_____

_____

_____

_____

_____

_____

_____

_____

_____

_____

THINGS
TO THINK
ABOUT

Do you have all the things you really need?

Do all the children of the world have
everything they need?

Do you have things you don't really need?

Here are the Ten Commandments. Read them carefully.

1. I am Adonai your God.
2. You shall have no other god beside Me.
3. You shall not take the Name of God in vain.
4. Remember the Sabbath day to keep it holy.
5. Honor your father and your mother.
6. You shall not murder.
7. You shall not commit adultery.
8. You shall not steal.
9. You shall not bear false witness.
10. You shall not covet.

You may have noticed that the first four of the Ten Commandments talk about how we should act with God. The others tell how we should act toward other people. The Fifth Commandment about honoring our parents is in the middle. It is like a bridge between the two kinds of Commandments.

Look at all ten again.

The Ten Commandments have very few words, but they say a great deal.

They talk to us about what we should think and believe, talk and say, act and do, every day, in every way, with God and with other people.

And when we listen to what the Ten Commandments have to say and are careful about what we think, say and do, in every way, every day, with everyone, and with God, we become very special people. We are keeping the promise our people made to God long ago near Mount Sinai—the promise to learn and keep the Ten Commandments.

FROM THE TALMUD

Before God gave the Ten Commandments to us, the Jewish people, God wanted a proof that we would honor and keep them.

We offered our leaders and princes as proof that we would learn and keep God's laws. But God would not accept our leaders and princes as proof.

So the Jewish people offered rabbis and teachers as proof that we would keep the Ten Commandments. But God would not accept our rabbis and teachers as proof.

Then we offered our children. We promised that our children and our children's children would learn and keep the Ten Commandments forever and ever.

That was the proof that God wanted. Because of the proof and that promise, God gave the Ten Commandments to the Jewish people.

May this book help you keep this promise, and be that proof.

THINGS TO THINK ABOUT

On the Ten Commandments at right, draw:

A Jewish star next to the commandments that tell us about how we behave toward God;

The word "shalom" next to the commandments that tell us how to behave toward other people.

1 I am Adonai your God.

2 You shall have no other god beside Me.

3 You shall not take the Name of God in vain.

4 Remember the Sabbath day to keep it holy.

5 Honor your father and your mother.

6 You shall not murder.

7 You shall not commit adultery.

8 You shall not steal.

9 You shall not bear false witness.

10 You shall not covet.

Sometimes a good deed helps us keep more than one of the Ten Commandments. For example, when we help our parents clean the house before Shabbat, we are keeping the commandment to honor our parents, *and* the commandment to remember the Sabbath day to keep it holy.

Which of the Ten Commandments do the following good deeds help us to keep? Write the number of the commandment in the box.

Helping our parents clean the house before Shabbat ☐

☐ Helping a poor person find a job

Becoming bar or bat mitzvah ☐

☐ Helping a friend study the kiddush

Instead of wanting our friend's toys, sharing our toys with them ☐

☐ Praying in the synagogue on Shabbat

Learning and keeping the Ten Commandments ☐

☐ Calling the police if you see someone robbing a house

Keeping a promise ☐

☐ Telling the truth

Going to Hebrew school ☐

☐ Running an errand for our grandparents

Thanking God for what we have ☐

CATEGORY SORT

Directions: The words or phrases listed below
tell about all Ten Commandments.
Write the number of the correct Commandment
next to each word or phrase.

_____ Promises made in God's Name

_____ Emunah

_____ No other gods

_____ Day of rest

_____ No adultery

_____ No coveting

_____ No false witness

_____ Keep the Sabbath Day holy

_____ Honor your father and mother

_____ No murder

_____ No stealing

_____ Pray

_____ Respect

_____ Vows

_____ One God

_____ Lies against someone else

_____ Lies that punish innocent people

_____ Wanting to take away something that someone else has

_____ Taking away something that someone else has

Look at the ten laws you wrote at the end of Chapter 1. Would you change that list now? How? Why?

_____

_____

_____

_____

_____

Can you recite the Ten Commandments by heart?

Would you like to live in a world without the Ten Commandments? _____

Why? _____

_____

_____

_____

_____

_____

In the space below, draw the proof God wanted before giving the Ten Commandments to the Jewish people. (Remember to include yourself in the picture!)